young CHANGEMAKERS
MAKING A
DIFFERENCE

Written By
STACY C. BAUER

D0963449

Illustrated By
MANUELA NTAMACK

This book is dedicated to Ava, Justin, Galilea, Jack, Mayli, Ryan, Kalia, Bishop, Kate, Felix, Winter and William. May your stories inspire others the way they have inspired me.

Making a Difference
Young Change Makers
Published by Hop Off the Press, LLC
www.stacycbauer.com

Minneapolis, MN

Book design by Travis D. Peterson.

Library of Congress Control Number: 2021911697
Bauer, Stacy C. Author
Ntamack, Emanuela Illustrator
Making a Difference

ISBN (Hardcover): 978-1-7373890-0-2
ISBN (Softcover): 978-1-7373890-4-0

JUVENILE NONFICTION

All inquiries of this book can be sent to the author.
For more information, please visit **www.stacycbauer.com**

MEET THE CHANGE MAKERS!

ANIMAL AMBASSADORS
Helping and advocating for animals.

CONSERVATION CREW
Saving the planet.

INSPIRING ICONS
Chasing their dreams and
encouraging others to do the same!

HELPING HANDS
Delivering support to those in need.

AVA

North Carolina, USA

INSPIRATIONAL ICONS

"BELIEVE IN
YOURSELF
AND BE
THE GENIUS
YOU ARE!"

For some kids, school can be tough. Things don't always come easily the first time you learn them. Ava Simmons knows firsthand what it feels like to struggle in school, especially with reading and math. When she was in second grade, she was teased for being behind the rest of her classmates. Ava was frustrated and wanted to quit, but she refused to give up on herself. Instead, Ava decided to change the world! She took her love of creating and experimenting to YouTube to inspire other kids not to give up, especially when things are hard!

Ava posted her first video, *How to Make Hand Sanitizer at Home During the Pandemic* in June 2020. Since then, she's made over twenty videos that have been viewed by more than 500,000 people around the world!

Making these videos has helped Ava as well. Not only is she having fun doing what she loves (experimenting and inspiring kids), but she's been learning! Ava has to study every day in order to find new content and write scripts for her videos. She researches S.T.E.M. (Science, Technology, Engineering, and Mathematics) books for ideas and tries to make everyday learning fun and exciting, so it doesn't feel like work.

Ava's hard work has paid off: she is now up to grade level in reading and math! More importantly, she feels good about herself and her new purpose: helping others.

Ava plans to keep sharing her love of S.T.E.M. with the world. She wants to build a S.T.E.M. Academy to help others develop unique and hidden talents, and to find their own passion!

AVA'S FUN FACTS:

- Ava loves sour things like lemons and pickles.
- Her favorite experiment is launching acid-base reaction rockets.
- She absolutely adores large Lego kits!

Periodic Table of the Elements

BECOME A

young
CHANGEMAKERS™
INSPIRATIONAL
ICON!

- Instead of giving up when things are hard, keep working!
- If you see others giving up, encourage them to keep going.
- Take something you love and use it to help others.
- Find out more about Ava here: www.teamgeniussquad.com

AVA'S ADVICE FOR YOU:

Identify what you are good at and zero in on those talents. Believe in yourself and transfer all of your focus and energy on your newly-discovered inner genius.

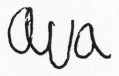

"Frogs breathe and drink through their skin, so they are sensitive to their environment. Scientists say that frogs are an indicator species. This means the frogs are telling us the world needs our help."–Justin

Do you have a favorite animal? Justin Sather loves frogs. He's loved them for as long as he can remember, which was why he was so upset to learn that nearly one-third of all frog species on the planet are on the verge of extinction. Chemicals are destroying their habitats. Justin knew this was a sign our planet needed help!

RESERVA YOUTH COUNCIL empowers young people to make a difference for threatened species and habitats through conservation, education, and storytelling.

Inspired by the book *What Do You Do With an Idea?* Justin founded For the Love of Frogs and started spreading the word about plastics, pollution, and **conservation**. He started out raising money by selling toy frogs, then thought of other ways to raise money. Justin has raised over $25,000 to help his favorite animal and donated all of the money to conservation groups.

Justin is also a member of the **Reserva Youth Council**, a group of youth who share a love of nature and want to protect it. Currently he has raised enough money to purchase and

JUSTIN'S FUN FACTS:

- He loves playing baseball and soccer.
- Justin's favorite frogs are Strawberry Dart Frogs, Mossy Frogs, and Glass Frogs.

protect over twenty acres of land in Ecuador! He is participating in the Million Letter Campaign: for every letter written, Rainforest Trust will match $3 toward the purchase of 244 acres of land in the Choco Rainforest of Ecuador. Every letter written will protect a classroom-sized area of rainforest!

To prevent mass extinctions and help with climate change, scientists warn that we must protect at least 30 percent of our lands, rivers, lakes, and wetlands by 2030. Justin has made reaching that 30 percent his goal; he wants to help protect the planet for his friends, family, the next generation, and, of course, the frogs.

JUSTIN'S ADVICE FOR YOU:

Start off with a small idea and then get bigger and bigger. Be brave, stay determined, and change the world!

Justin

BECOME A young CHANGEMAKERS™ ANIMAL AMBASSADOR!

- Get involved in the Million Letter Campaign! Write a letter about your love of nature and why it's important to protect it.

- Visit www.fortheloveoffrogs.com to get a free template and to find out where to send your letter.

Frog photos by Santiago Ron are licensed under CC BY-ND 2.0.

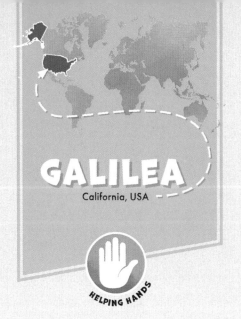

"UNICORNS ARE MAGICAL, BRAVE, AND COURAGEOUS, JUST LIKE YOU."

Meet Galilea Gonzalez, a girl who is spreading happiness through stuffed unicorns! Galilea was only six years old when her grandfather was hospitalized. When she saw how much a picture she'd drawn of a unicorn cheered him up, she decided to do something to cheer up many more people.

Galilea learned how to make her own bath salts at a Girl Scout event. She sells the bath salts at local events and uses the money to purchase plush unicorns for sick kids at local hospitals. Galilea's Unicorn Project has been recognized nationally: she is the recipient of Disney Channel's Lead like Elena award, and she has earned a Reflecting Excellence award from *Reflejos*, a bilingual newspaper in Chicago. Galilea hopes to keep bringing joy to children through the magic of unicorns.

GALILEA'S FUN FACTS:

- Galilea loves sushi! She could live off of sushi and beef jerky.

- Galilea's favorite place is the French Quarter in New Orleans.

- Galilea's dog Luna has been with her almost all her life. Luna sleeps with her and goes with her everywhere.

11

BECOME A young CHANGEMAKERS™ HELPING HAND!

- Make and deliver cards to sick children or others at hospitals in your area.

- Visit Galilea's Facebook page and donate to her cause! Follow: @magicofunicornsgalilea

GALILEA'S ADVICE FOR YOU:
Always be yourself and never give up.

Galilea

 12

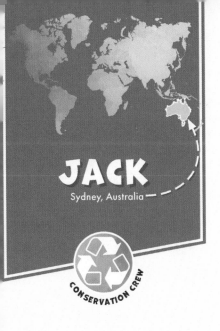

JACK

Sydney, Australia

CONSERVATION CREW

"YOU MAY BE SMALL, BUT YOUR VOICE IS MIGHTY!"

Those are the words of Jack Berne, a boy from Sydney, Australia, who is doing what he can to help the environment. A few years ago, his area of Australia was experiencing a severe drought. Farmers were losing crops and selling their animals (they weren't able to feed them) due to lack of rain. After watching a Kid's News program about the drought, Jack decided to do something. He brainstormed with his parents, and A Fiver for a Farmer was born!

Jack's program asked kids to dress up as farmers and bring $5 to school. The money would go toward helping farmers pay to feed their animals and bring in water for their crops.

But Jack didn't stop with his own school. He wrote an email to some local media (television stations, radio stations, and newspapers), asking them to help share his idea. The very next day, Jack appeared live on television! His family set up a GoFundMe page to collect donations and a website to spread the word. Their goal was to raise $20,000. Jack blew that target out of the water, reaching his target in just fourteen hours! Five weeks after his launch, A Fiver for a Farmer had raised a whopping one million dollars!

Jack has seen firsthand how loud your voice can be. Just because you're young doesn't mean you can't make a difference!

Jack has also created Mail Mates. Through Mail Mates, people around Australia will be connected to each other through letter writing, just like pen pals. Jack knows that sometimes kids can feel alone. He hopes that Mail Mates will give them a place to talk about whatever they want, in a way that makes them feel safe about sharing their feelings.

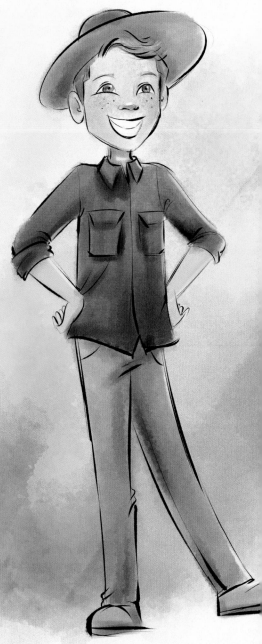

 14

JACK'S FUN FACTS:

- Jack's favorite food is Ramen.
- He has a rabbit named BunBun.
- He loves having family holidays with his cousins.
- His least favorite food is mushrooms.
- His favorite thing about school is playing sports! Jack loves basketball and rugby.

BECOME A

young CHANGEMAKERS™ CONSERVATION CREW MEMBER!

- **Find out if there are any environmental concerns in your area and what you can do to help.**
- **Be kind to the Earth. Turn off water when you're not using it. Pick up litter. Recycle.**
- **Write a kind letter to someone.**

JACK'S ADVICE FOR YOU:

Get out there. Use your voice, make a difference, do something for someone else. I promise this will be more rewarding than anything else. Spreading kindness is cool! Watching someone's frown turn to a smile because of something you did is like a superpower that everyone has in them. And when in doubt, move your body... that always helps me!

Jack

MAYLI
Texts, USA

INSPIRATIONAL ICONS

"I CAN DO ANYTHING I WANT TO. I JUST DO IT A LITTLE DIFFERENTLY."

These are the words of Mayli Gibson, a determined and joyful girl from Texas, in the United States. Mayli was born with spina bifida. That means her spine and spinal cord didn't form properly. Mayli uses a wheelchair to get around, but that has never held her back!

When Mayli was four years old, her family contacted their local parks and **advocated** for **inclusive** playground equipment. They wanted all kids to be able to play together. They were able to get an inclusive park built in their town, and the other playground was updated with **accessible** equipment. Their school district also replaced all seven of their playgrounds! Mayli and her family want to raise awareness so that in the future people won't make their businesses, homes, and playgrounds accessible because they *have* to, but because they *want* to.

But Mayli's successes aren't limited to making play spaces accessible. Mayli is very active. She loves basketball, track-and-field, and dance. And she wants to make all kinds of recreation accessible. When her family couldn't find a wheelchair dance team, they started one themselves! Being at the same eye level as their peers, with whom they have a lot in common, has given the girls on the dance team a newfound confidence and changed their lives for the better.

Now, Mayli's family is hoping to grow the dance team in order to reach kids all over the world!

Mayli wants to continue to spread the importance of inclusion and accessibility. When she is older, she would like to become a physical therapist or a doctor to help kids like herself.

MAYLI'S FUN FACTS:

- Mayli loves to sing and is taking voice lessons.
- She loves horses, and dreams of having one of her own some day.
- She enjoys making slime.

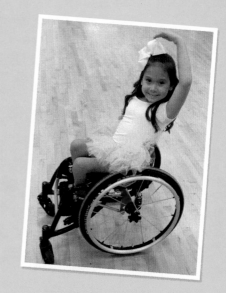

An accessible playground makes sure people with wheelchairs are able to use it. An inclusive playground allows children of all abilities to play together. (Photo above by Tdorante10 is licensed under CC BY-SA 4.0)

young CHANGEMAKERS™
INSPIRATIONAL ICON!

- Are the playgrounds in your area inclusive to all kids? If not, talk to your family about how to change that!

- Read more about Mayli on Instagram! Follow: @mayligibson

MAYLI'S ADVICE FOR YOU:

Your voice matters! Use it to speak up for what is right. No matter your age or ability, you *can* be a changemaker.

Mayli

RYAN

California, USA

CONSERVATION CREW

"IF A KID LIKE ME CAN DO IT, YOU CAN TOO!"

Did you know that in 2017, only 66 percent of **discarded** paper and cardboard, 27 percent of glass, and 8 percent of plastics were recycled in the United States? The rest ended up in **landfills** and even the ocean! One young changemaker in California decided to do something about it!

When Ryan Hickman was three years old, his dad brought him to the recycling center. Ryan was so inspired by what he saw that he asked his neighbors to start recycling instead of throwing things in the garbage. He even brought them bags so they could save their recyclables for him. He then collected the items, sorted them, and took them to be recycled.

But for Ryan, collecting bottles in his own neighborhood wasn't enough. He wanted to educate and inspire others to recycle and help clean up the planet. He started a recycling program at his school and now has hundreds of local "customers" who call him each week to pick up their recycling. He even started his own company when he was five, **Ryan's Recycling Company**, which has now recycled over one million cans and bottles! His family lives near the beach, so when Ryan isn't sorting recyclables, he picks up litter left on the beach.

Now, he travels around the world speaking at events,

hoping to educate people about the importance of taking care of the planet. Ryan hopes to grow his company into a bigger organization in the future. He wants to keep cleaning up the Earth and inspiring others to help!

Discarded (used) paper that's thrown in the garbage goes to the landfill. A landfill is a large hole where garbage is dumped and buried. A better place for used paper to go is to the recycling center, where it can be made into new paper and used again!

RYAN'S FUN FACTS:

- Ryan plays violin and collects coins.
- Ryan's least favorite food is tomatoes.
- He loves math and helping his mom cook.

- Educate yourself about recycling and commit to recycling things each week!
- Offer to help your neighbors with their recycling.
- Pick up litter in your area.
- Learn more about Ryan's mission at www.ryansrecycling.com

RYAN'S ADVICE FOR YOU:

So many kids don't know that they have the ability to make a difference in the world. Just follow your dreams, stay focused and don't be afraid to take chances.

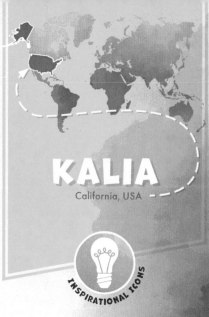

KALIA
California, USA

"LET'S MAKE HISTORY!"

Young people can change the world! That's the message Kalia Love Jones, the youngest filmmaker ever to have a film nominated for an NAACP Image Award, wants you to hear.

Her animated short film *The Power of Hope* shares an inspirational message of overcoming obstacles and hardships.

Kalia always knew she wanted to be a filmmaker, and when

THE POWER OF HOPE
ANIMATED SHORT FILM

she heard former First Lady Michelle Obama's speech about how young people can change the world, she decided to take action! Kalia wanted to create a film that would motivate young people to follow their dreams. When she was twelve years old, Kalia started by writing out story ideas for her film. She even created the 2D character designs. At age thirteen, she began preproduction – putting together a team of people to help her produce the film. For her, this was the hardest part of the process, since she didn't know anyone in the industry, how to find them, or even who she needed.

But that wasn't her biggest challenge. Kalia lacked the confidence needed to go out and ask for help. She was filled with doubt as to whether she could accomplish her goal. Luckily, she wasn't alone. With her father by her side, they went where they thought they could find people eager to help produce the film:

college campuses. Nervous, Kalia waited until class was out, then approached college students and pitched her idea. Being so young, it was hard to get people to take her seriously, but she didn't give up. She found **animators**, **music producers**, **sound mixers**, and **artists**. Kalia had to use money from her savings, birthdays, and even money she made from recycling to pay for production, but she was willing to do it.

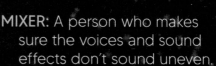

MUSIC PRODUCER: A person who works on the songs and music in a film.

MIXER: A person who makes sure the voices and sound effects don't sound uneven.

ARTIST: A person who works on character designs and other artwork. Kalia's artist worked on changing her 2D character designs to 3D for the film.

ANIMATOR: A person who brings the artist's characters to life and gives them movement.

- Her favorite food is spaghetti.
- Her least favorite food is fish.
- She likes to play the piano and the flute in her spare time.

The NAACP (National Association for the Advancement of Colored People) was formed in 1909. It is a group that works to make sure everyone in the United States has equal rights.

Once she found her team, Kalia got to work. The entire project took her approximately two years from start to finish! Once it was completed, she entered it into Oscar-qualifying film festivals. Her film received a lot of praise and was nominated for numerous awards!

The experience of making her film and seeing the effect it had on people has given Kalia more confidence and has solidified her desire to continue in filmmaking. Through this film, Kalia was able to inspire her community to believe that they are never too young to achieve greatness. She plans to continue working and directing in animation, and one day hopes to own her own animation studio.

BECOME A young CHANGEMAKERS™ INSPIRATIONAL ICON!

- Don't give up on your dreams! Take your passion and find a way to bring it to life!
- Encourage others to follow their dreams.

KALIA'S ADVICE FOR YOU:

Believe in yourself and go for your dreams.

Kalia

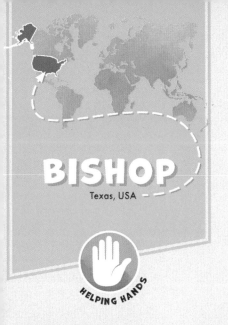

BISHOP
Texas, USA

HELPING HANDS

"I DON'T THINK BABIES SHOULD DIE IN HOT CARS."

When Bishop Curry was ten years old, a baby who lived down the street from him passed away because she was accidentally left in a hot car. She was only six months old. Bishop was inspired to create something that would stop that from happening again.

the programming (the code that told the Oasis how to do its job). He then had to apply for a **patent** – a piece of paper that would stop others from copying his idea.

After receiving the patent, Bishop worked with a small engineering company to build the **functional prototype device**. His future goal is to get Oasis into stores and into the hands of parents everywhere.

The first thing he did was draw up the plans for his invention. He called it Oasis. Bishop describes Oasis as a device designed to prevent small children from dying in hot cars. It would be attached to the child's car seat and would identify if a child has been left in a car seat at a time when the car is stopped or is heating up. In the event of this, the device blows cold air on the child and calls their parents. If parents do not respond, Oasis contacts the police.

Once Bishop designed his plans, he made a clay model. After that, he purchased plastic and electronic parts and made a rough **prototype** out of clay. His father helped him with

Bishop's device has the potential to save lives and prevent tragic deaths. He believes in the power of science to change the world, and has given talks about not letting age and lack of resources limit your dreams.

BRAINSTORM: Think of and list ideas.

PROTOTYPE: A model or example of your invention.

PATENT: A piece of paper that shows you have registered your idea with the government. It stops others from copying your idea.

FUNCTIONAL PROTOTYPE DEVICE: A working model of your invention.

BECOME A

young CHANGEMAKERS™ HELPING HAND!

- **You can be an inventor!**

- **Identify a problem, brainstorm solutions, and start designing your invention!**

IDENTIFY A PROBLEM	BRAINSTORM SOLUTIONS	SKETCH OUT YOUR IDEA	CREATE A PROTOTYPE
TEST IT OUT	MAKE CORRECTIONS	GET IT PRODUCED	INTRODUCE IT TO THE WORLD!

BISHOP'S ADVICE FOR YOU:
Hard work always equals success.

Bishop

KATE

Texas, USA

ANIMAL AMBASSADORS

"ADVOCACY HAS NO AGE LIMIT."

Seven-year-old Kate Gilman Williams was inspired to take action after going on a trip to Africa. While on **safari**, she met a knowledgeable and passionate **game driver** named Michelle who told her that humans are the reason African animals are facing extinction. Kate was shocked and upset to learn that every fifteen minutes an elephant is killed for its tusks, and every eight hours a rhino is killed for its horn. She was even more upset when she discovered that there are only two white rhinos left in the entire world!

Inspired, Kate asked Michelle if she would write a book with her. They spent months emailing ideas back and forth. The book really took off when it was endorsed by **Dr. Jane Goodall**, Angela Sheldrick of The Sheldrick Wildlife Trust, and Brian Sheth of Global Wildlife Conservation. Kate and Michelle donate *all* profits from their book to the three partners who had supported them along the way. But Kate wasn't done advocating for the animals. She launched a website and created a presentation kids can use at their own schools. She even started her own business, **Kids Can Save Animals**, to show kids that they can be animal advocates, too! Kate loves letting other children know that they can make a difference, no matter their age!

"I founded Kids Can Save Animals to help my generation turn their natural love for animals and our planet into **advocacy**. I believe that advocacy has no age limit. And the truth is, it is up to my generation to fix big things."

Kate wanted to teach other kids just like her what they need to know to help save the elephants and mend the planet, so she partnered with Project 15 from Microsoft to create Club 15. Her club connects top scientists, conservationists, and technologists with kids and teens so they can take action to save wildlife and wild spaces 15 minutes at a time. Each episode of her vlog features a video from people who are saving our planet. They share what can be done now to join the fight.

In the future, Kate plans to continue advocating and raising awareness about helping animals and our planet.

Jane Goodall is a scientist who spent over sixty years advocating for animals–especially chimpanzees–and the environment. In fact, she even lived with them for a time! In 1991, she started Roots and Shoots, an environmental service program for young people.

KATE'S FUN FACTS:

- Kate enjoys volleyball.
- She likes acting.
- Kate loves visiting Africa.

 30

BECOME A

young CHANGEMAKERS™ ANIMAL AMBASSADOR!

- **Learn how you can advocate for animals.**
- **Visit kidscansaveanimals.com and join Club 15.**

KATE'S ADVICE FOR YOU:

We may be young, but age does not define our impact. To make a difference, we simply need to take action.

Kate

FELIX
Uffing, Germany

CONSERVATION CREW

"CHILDREN CAN MAKE A DIFFERENCE.
ONE MOSQUITO CANNOT DO ANYTHING AGAINST
A RHINO, BUT A THOUSAND MOSQUITOES CAN
MAKE A RHINO CHANGE ITS DIRECTION."

Have you ever planted a tree? Can you imagine planting a million trees? It would be almost impossible to do on your own, but a group of caring individuals can accomplish great things. When Felix Finkbeiner was in fourth grade, his teacher asked him to create and present a project about **climate change**. Felix started researching the subject and learned about Professor Wangari Maathai, an African woman who, together with other women, planted 30 million trees over the course of thirty years! Inspired, Felix decided to take action. He set a goal to plant a million trees in countries around the world.

Just a few weeks later, Felix and his classmates planted the first tree in front of their school near Munich, Germany. Local reporters shared their project. More and more schools joined his movement, which he named **Plant-for-the-Planet**. As the movement grew, Felix and his family realized they needed help. His principal, teacher, and lots of students from his school stepped up. Some high school students made a website for his new company. More than 100 students sent letters to other schools. In just three years, children from 93 countries around the world helped Plant-for-the-Planet reach their goal of one million trees planted! But Felix didn't stop with just a website. Although he was only in elementary school, he spoke in front of thousands of businesspeople, scientists, and other adults. He was nervous, but he pushed forward because of his passion for trees.

At a **Plant-for-the-Planet Academy**, children learn about the climate crisis. They hear from children who are already involved in the project about what they can do to develop their own projects. They learn to give presentations and how to organize planting parties.

FELIX'S FUN FACTS:

- Felix enjoys mountain biking and swimming in the summer.

- In the winter, he goes snowboarding and skiing.

- He loves spending time with friends.

Ten years after it started, Plant-for-the-Planet had established more than 1,000 **academies**, or schools, in 71 countries, empowering young members to learn about climate change, the importance of tree-planting, and how to take action.

Plant-for-the-Planet is still going strong, with a current goal of planting a trillion trees worldwide.

So far, Plant-for-the-Planet youths have planted more than 13.5 billion trees worldwide, well on their way to achieving that goal.

Felix never expected that his idea would become so powerful, but he has shown that with determination, courage, and support from others, one boy can make a difference!

"STOP TALKING, START PLANTING." –Plant-for-the-Planet

Girls at a Plant-for-the-Planet Academy in Bhimavaram, India, are making plans for how to motivate people to contribute to the Trillion Tree Campaign. (Photo used with permission by Plant-for-the-Planet.)

FELIX'S ADVICE FOR YOU:
Stop talking, start planting! Figure out the problem, then take action.

BECOME A

young
CHANGEMAKERS™
CONSERVATION CREW MEMBER!

- **Plant a tree! Organize a tree planting party in your community.**

- **Learn more about how Felix's company raises money for plants and chooses the trees here: www.plant-for-the-planet.org You will also have the opportunity to donate some money to have a tree planted!**

Felix

33

Winter Noel Joy is a girl who is as unique as her name. Winter's name was inspired by the day she was supposed to be born: Christmas. Even though she came early, on December 16, her mother kept her name as a reminder of when she was due.

When Winter was about six years old, she started coming home from school crying, because she was being bullied about her hair. Her mother tried styling her hair differently, but it made no difference. After many long talks with her mother, Winter started making a prayer blanket to give hope and encouragement to those who are being bullied, like she was.

Winter collected fabric squares from other children at churches, schools, and events. Each square had a prayer from the child written on it. Winter wants every child to feel included and loved. She believes making a prayer square will encourage kids to find quiet time to meditate and think happy thoughts.

The idea of Winter's prayer blanket has since grown into a "digital love square" project. Children all over the world have begun making prayer squares and sharing them via social media using unique hashtags. The purpose is to spread positivity, kindness, compassion, and love.

WINTER'S FUN FACTS:

- Winter loves the harp. Every year she asks for one for Christmas.

- Winter has an older sister twice her age.

- She enjoys painting and photography.

BECOME A

young CHANGEMAKERS™
HELPING HAND!

- If you see someone being teased, say something! Tell the person teasing them to stop or go get an adult.

- Make your own love square with your prayer, hope, or dream written on it. Have your parents post a photo of you and your love square using the hashtags #prayerchangesthingschallenge or #lovechangesthingschallenge.

- Be kind to everyone.

WINTER'S ADVICE FOR YOU:

Start small: first change yourself, then your home, then your extended family, then your community, then the world. The key is to just start.

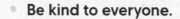

Many people tell stories with words, but did you know that you can also tell stories through music? That's exactly what William Zhang, a young piano prodigy from the United States, does.

When William was five, he performed at his school. Afterwards, many people approached him, praising and thanking him for playing. Listening to how much they had all loved hearing him play, William decided right then and there to use his talent to bring happiness to others. His parents started contacting nursing homes, senior centers, and churches, all of which welcomed him to come perform.

At age six, William entered the American Protégé International Piano and String Competition. Around 1,000 competitive musicians aged 5–56 from 17 countries submitted videos of their piano skills, and William took the top spot! His win earned him the chance to perform at Carnegie Hall.

CARNEGIE HALL
Located in New York, Carnegie Hall is the most prestigious – or famous – concert stage in the United States.

Although William has a natural talent for the piano, he knows that being great takes work. He spends time practicing every day and takes weekly lessons.

But William doesn't just play the music written by others. He **composes**, or writes, his own music, and loves experimenting with sounds and capturing new melodies:

"I let my mind drift away into a dream, in a field where there are flowers and a picnic. The melo-

WILLIAM'S FUN FACTS:

- He enjoys reading and drawing.

- His favorite composer is Mozart. He imagines fun stories in Mozart's cheerful compositions.

- Willam will release his first album featuring his original compositions soon!

- He aspires to be a concert pianist and classical music composer.

- His favorite foods are dumplings with pork and chives made by his dad, and Starbursts.

- He loves playing outside with the ducks at the lake.

dies will slowly creep out of their hiding spots. My brain will then act like a SWAT team, but not a real one, then it will arrest the melodies."

William enjoys using his talents to introduce other kids to music –especially classical music. He wants to inspire other kids like him to learn an instrument, because he believes more kids falling in love with music will make the world a better place.

For him, playing piano is a chance to tell a story. When he sits down to compose a song, he plays a little, then pauses to tell the story to his parents. Then he plays some more and shares more about the story. One particular story William tells is about a little oven-bird who wants to chirp, but keeps burping instead. Despite being teased by other birds, the ovenbird doesn't give up. He practices every day until at last, he learns how to chirp!

William believes that if you are dedicated and work hard, you will eventually succeed in singing a beautiful song, just like the little ovenbird. Then, the whole world will hear your voice.

BECOME A young CHANGEMAKERS™ INSPIRATIONAL ICON!

- Share your special talent with others!
- Make cards or paint rocks or pictures for people!
- Bake cookies for a neighbor.
- Find a way to share your musical talent with others!

WILLIAM'S ADVICE FOR YOU:

Have a dream and don't give up. Let the world hear your voice just like the little ovenbird.

William

STACY C. BAUER

A native of Minneapolis, MN, Stacy C. Bauer is a wife, teacher, mother of two and owner of Hop Off the Press – a publisher of quality children's books. Along with self publishing her own books, Stacy enjoys helping aspiring authors realize their dreams. She is hoping to inspire people around the world to make a difference with her newest endeavor, nonfiction book series *Young Change Makers*. For more information and to check out Stacy's other books including her children's picture books, visit www.stacycbauer.com.

EMANUELA NTAMACK

Emanuela Ntamack is an artist and children's book illustrator, a beloved wife and mother. She is married to her Cameroonian husband Alix, and together they have two boys. She has been drawing continuously ever since she could hold a pencil. Growing up, she studied Art and Design in school and university. After she became a mother, she discovered her love for children's books illustrations. One of the biggest satisfactions of her work is when children- including her own- are inspired by the illustrations that she creates. She is thankful to God for the gift of art, and for the diversity and the beauty of Creation, which is a never-ending source of inspiration.

YOU CAN MAKE A DIFFERENCE!

We all have unique gifts and strengths. How can you use
your one-of-a-kind strengths to make a difference?

My unique gifts and strengths include: (These can include things such as
playing an instrument, cooking, painting, public speaking, being friendly...)

_____

_____

_____

_____

_____

_____

I am passionate about: (a certain animal(s), helping small children or the
elderly, helping the environment in some way)

_____

_____

_____

_____

_____

_____

MY IDEAS

Things I can do to use my strengths to make a difference in an area I am passionate about:

_____

_____

_____

_____

_____

_____

_____

_____

_____

_____

_____

_____

_____

_____

MY ACTION PLAN

My idea/goal: _____

_____

_____

My first step: _____

_____

_____

Who I can ask for help if I need it: _____

_____

_____

What I need to get started: _____

_____

_____

My ultimate goal: _____

_____

_____

YOU *CAN* DO THIS! YOU'RE NEVER TOO YOUNG TO MAKE A DIFFERENCE!

Made in United States
Orlando, FL
09 December 2022

25573647R00024